THE ILLUSTRATED
ENCYCLOPEDIA

VOLUME 2

Belitha Press

First published 1995 by
Macmillan Education Australia Pty Ltd

First published in the United Kingdom in 1995 by
Belitha Press Limited
31 Newington Green, London N16 9PU

Cataloguing in print data available from the British Library.

ISBN 1 85561 521 5 (Vol 2)
ISBN 1 85561 529 0 (Set)

Consultant: Frances Warhurst
UK editor: Maria O'Neill
Project editor: Jo Higgins

Typeset by Polar Design
Printed in Hong Kong

Acknowledgements

The author and publisher are grateful to the following for permission to reproduce copyright photographs:

A.A.P. Photo Library, p. 42 (bottom); Abbington Dolls, p. 58 (top); Kevin Aitken/A.N.T. Photo Library, p. 59; Bureau of
Meteorology, p. 31 (top centre); Coo-ee Picture Library, pp. 7 (bottom), 10 (top left), 11, 13 (left), 15, 23 (top), 24, 26, 28, 29
(left), 30 (top right), 36, 38, 40, 43, 44 (top & bottom right), 49 (bottom), 60, 64 (bottom), 54 (bottom), 56, 61 (bottom);
GBRMPA, p. 37 (top); International Photographic Library, p. 10 (bottom); N.H.P.A./A.N.T. Photo Library, p. 47 (bottom left &
right); Northside Photographics, pp. 9 (bottom), 10 (right), 13 (right), 14 (top), 23 (left & bottom), 25 (top), 29 (right), 31
(bottom), 44 (left/N. Rowe), 49 (top/Patrick Horton), 51, 54 (top), 55 (bottom), 57 (Dianne Bloomfield), 63 (top); Owens-
Corning, p. 25 (bottom left); Queensland Museum, p. 52; 10 Network, p. 14 (bottom); Otto Rogge/A.N.T. Photo Library, p. 17,
20 (bottom); Royal Victorian Eye & Ear Hospital, p. 55 (top); Silvestris/A.N.T. Photo Library, p. 47 (top); Village Roadshow, p. 9
(centre right).

While every care has been taken to trace and acknowledge copyright, the publishers tender their apologies for any accidental
infringement where copyright has proved untraceable.

Illustrators

Sharyn Madder: 6, 7, 16, 17, 18, 19, 40, 46, 47, 49, 56, 57, 59, 64
Rhyll Plant: 12, 20, 21, 26, 27, 29, 32, 33, 36, 37, 61
John Fairbridge: 4, 5, 13, 15, 22, 24, 28, 34, 35, 38, 39, 43, 58, 63
Paul Konye: 8, 9, 11, 14, 30, 31, 41, 42, 54, 55, 62
Andrew Plant: 53
Xiangyi Mo: 48, 50, 51
Chantal Stewart: 45, 60

HOW TO USE THIS BOOK

The Illustrated Encyclopedia has over 300 entries. The entries are arranged alphabetically. To find your topic, use the guide letters at the top of each page to check you have the right volume. The first letter of your topic will be highlighted.

TOPIC: CALENDAR

guide letter

A B C D E F G H I J K L M

Use the guide words printed in the top right-hand corner of each page to find your topic. The guide words list the entries on a double-page spread. They are listed alphabetically. Check the guide words to see if you need to go backwards or forwards.

guide word

CALENDAR

You can also use the index in Volume 9 to find your topic.

calendar
  Volume 2   **4 – 5**
  Volume 5   56 – 57

If you cannot find your topic in its alphabetical order in the encyclopedia, use the index.

car
  see motor car
  see transport
  see wheel

TOPIC: CAR

The index lists all the topics in alphabetical order. It tells you where you will find your topic.

More information on how to use the encyclopedia and the index can be found in Volume 9.

CALENDAR

SEE ALSO
• Clock • Days of the Week
• Months of the Year • Moon

A calendar is a way of measuring time. Calendars measure time by days, weeks, months and years. The days, weeks, months and years are numbered so that people know when things are going to happen.

PARTS OF A CALENDAR

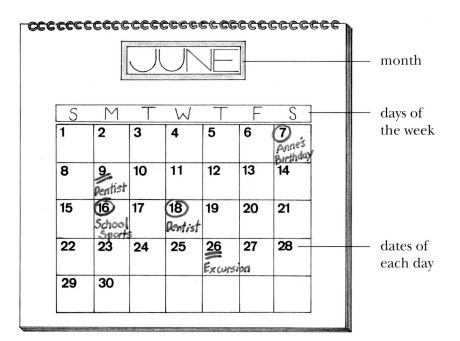

month

days of the week

dates of each day

One day is the time it takes the Earth to spin around once on its axis. This is called a solar day. One week is seven days.

1 day

One month is the time it takes the Moon to circle once around the Earth - about 29½ days. This is a lunar month.

Moon
Earth
29½ days

One year is the time it takes the Earth to go around the Sun. A solar year is 365¼ days long.

Earth
Sun
365¼ days

A LEAP YEAR

The Earth takes a little longer than 365 days to go around the Sun. Every four years, an extra day is added to February. This makes up for the quarter of a day which is not counted each year.

HISTORY

Long ago people made calendars:
- by counting the days and nights
- by watching the phases of the Moon
- by watching the seasons passing.

KINDS OF CALENDARS

There are three main kinds of calendars.
- Solar calendars are based on the solar year.
- Lunar calendars are based on the lunar month.
- Luni-solar calendars are a combination of the solar and lunar calendars.

ROMAN CALENDAR

Long ago, the Romans had a calendar where the year started in March. This was difficult for people to follow.

· · · · · · · · · · · · · · · · · ·

JULIAN CALENDAR

In about the year 46 BC, Emperor Julius Caesar began a new, simpler calendar which began on 1 January. One year did not quite match the time it takes for the Earth to move around the Sun.

· · · · · · · · · · · · · · · · · ·

GREGORIAN CALENDAR

Today, most people use the Gregorian calendar. It is a solar calendar and has 365 days which are divided into 12 months. The Gregorian calendar was started in 1582 when Pope Gregory XIII changed the Julian calendar to make it more exact.

5

CAMEL

SEE ALSO • Animal • Desert • Mammal • Ungulates

A camel is a mammal. It is a strong animal with one or two humps on its back. Camels usually live in the desert. A camel can go a long time with little food or water.

PARTS OF AN ARABIAN CAMEL

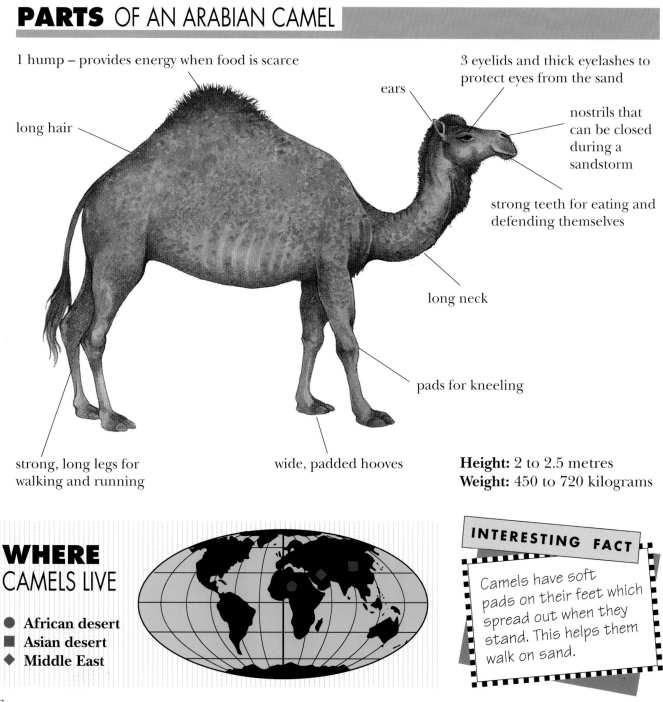

1 hump – provides energy when food is scarce

3 eyelids and thick eyelashes to protect eyes from the sand

ears

long hair

nostrils that can be closed during a sandstorm

strong teeth for eating and defending themselves

long neck

pads for kneeling

strong, long legs for walking and running

wide, padded hooves

Height: 2 to 2.5 metres
Weight: 450 to 720 kilograms

WHERE CAMELS LIVE

● **African desert**
■ **Asian desert**
◆ **Middle East**

INTERESTING FACT

Camels have soft pads on their feet which spread out when they stand. This helps them walk on sand.

KINDS OF CAMELS

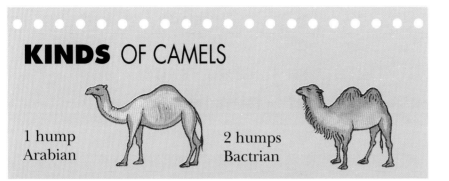

1 hump
Arabian

2 humps
Bactrian

HOW A CAMEL MOVES

A camel can walk slowly or run quickly. When a camel walks or runs, both legs on one side of its body move forward at the same time.

◀ A camel is a useful animal for people who live in the desert. Camels can be used for transport and food. Camels provide wool and leather which can be used for clothing and shelter.

FOOD

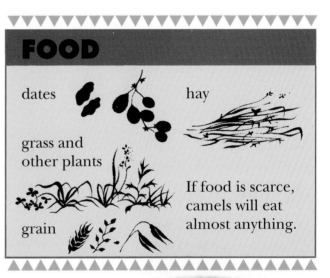

dates

hay

grass and other plants

grain

If food is scarce, camels will eat almost anything.

THE CAMEL FAMILY

alpaca

llama

guanaco

vicuna

HOW CAMELS LIVE

• A female camel usually has one calf at a time.
• A calf can stand and run when it is only a few hours old.
• It stays with its mother until it is four years old.

CAMERA

SEE ALSO | • Cartoon • Heritage • Light • Telescope • Television

A camera can take photographs. Cameras are box-shaped with a glass lens and a film inside.

PARTS OF A CAMERA

shutter-release button

wind-on lever

viewfinder

flash

lens

shutter to let light in

HOW A PHOTOGRAPH IS TAKEN

- You press the shutter-release button to take a photograph.
- The shutter opens quickly to let in light.
- The light touches the film and the image is recorded.

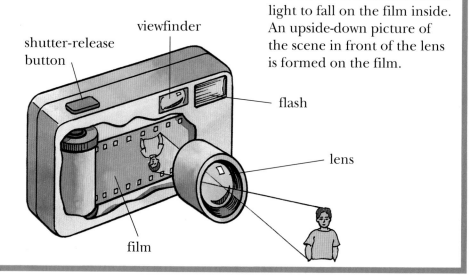

shutter-release button

viewfinder

flash

lens

film

The lens of the camera allows light to fall on the film inside. An upside-down picture of the scene in front of the lens is formed on the film.

FILM

You need to have a film in the camera to take photographs. When you have used up all the film, you take it out of the back of the camera. Special chemicals are used to develop and print the film.

film case goes
in here

HISTORY

Old photographs show us what people looked like and what they did in the past.

MOVIE CAMERAS ▶

A movie camera takes many photographs very quickly. When the photographs are shown in order through a projector, the images in the photographs seem to move.

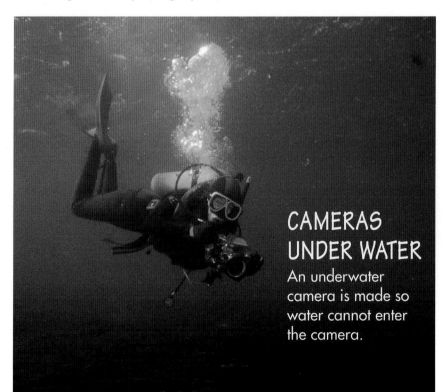

CAMERAS UNDER WATER

An underwater camera is made so water cannot enter the camera.

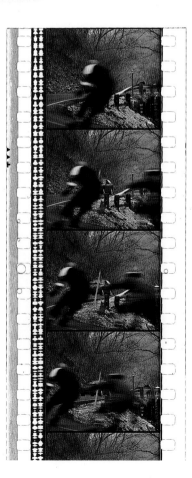

CAMOUFLAGE

SEE ALSO • Animal • Insect • Jaguars and Leopards • Lion

Camouflage disguises the shape, colour and pattern of something so it looks different. Camouflage makes an animal difficult to see. Camouflage protects animals from their enemies. It also helps some animals catch their food.

Some insects look like a twig or leaf. They trick their enemies.

Some snakes have a mottled skin. This helps them blend into their background.

▼ Military forces use camouflage in wars. They wear uniforms that are difficult to see.

A polar bear's white fur makes it hard to be seen in the snow.

INTERESTING FACT

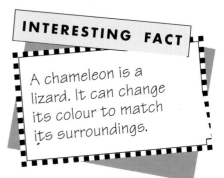

A chameleon is a lizard. It can change its colour to match its surroundings.

CAMPING

| SEE ALSO | • Conservation • House • National Park |

Camping is living outdoors. When you go camping, you can use a tent, a caravan, a cabin or sleep under the stars.

EQUIPMENT

penknife

hatchet or axe

cooking and eating tools

matches

first aid kit

sleeping bag

torch

comfortable and practical clothes

Hikers carry all they need for camping in packs on their backs.

KINDS OF TENTS

You can have large tents for lots of people or a small tent for one person.

large tent

small tent

CAMP SITE ▶

Choose a flat space near to water to pitch your tent.

◀ CAMPING RULE

Always leave your camp site as you found it.

11

CANARY

SEE ALSO • Animal • Bird • Pet

A canary is a small bird. It is a popular pet.
Canaries belong to the finch family of birds.

The first canaries came from the Canary Islands, off the coast of Africa.

Canary Islands

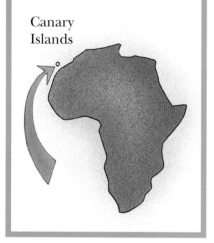

A PET CANARY

A canary needs:
* a large cage for flying
* its cage cleaned every day
* fresh drinking water every day
* fresh bath water every day
* fresh food every day.

FOOD

seed

green plants

cuttlefish shell

HOW CANARIES LIVE

In the wild, a canary's nest is made from dry moss and grass. It is built high in a tree. Canaries usually lay four to five eggs at a time.

Pet canaries are usually yellow, orange or a reddish yellow. Canaries can sing beautifully.

CANOE

SEE ALSO
• Boat • Floating • River
• Water Sports

A canoe is a long, narrow boat.
It has pointed ends and a curved bottom.
Paddles are used to steer and move the canoe in water.

PARTS OF A CANOE

Most canoes are 5 metres long
and 1 metre wide.

life jacket in case
you fall in the water

single-bladed paddle

HISTORY

Maori boat builders in New
Zealand carved their
canoes from tree trunks.
These canoes are called
dugout canoes.

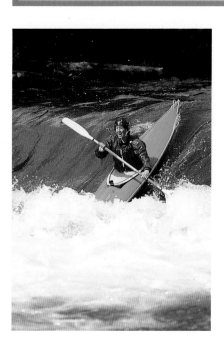

CANOEING AND KAYAKING

Canoeing and kayaking are exciting sports. Kayaks are canoes
that are covered-in. You use a double-bladed paddle to move
through the water. Canoeists use a single-bladed paddle and an
open canoe.

INTERESTING FACT

Inuits from the
Arctic use kayaks for
hunting and fishing.

CARTOON

SEE ALSO • Camera • Painting

A cartoon is a drawing that tells a story.
It can be a drawing with or without words.

A cartoonist is a ▶ person who draws cartoons. A comic strip is a number of cartoons which are joined together to tell a story.

AN ANIMATED CARTOON ▼

An animated cartoon is a series of drawings that are photographed on to film. The figures in each drawing are slightly different. When the film is played, the figures appear to move. Sound is added to make the figures speak.

DRAWING CARTOONS

If you want your character to speak, you can use speech balloons. You can use simple lines to show how a person feels.

CASTLE

SEE ALSO • Heritage • House • Knight

A castle is a building with high walls and towers. People built castles long ago to protect them from enemies. Many people lived and worked in a castle.

PARTS OF A CASTLE

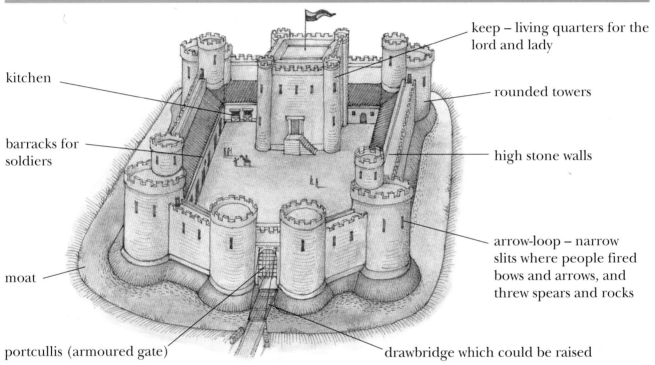

keep – living quarters for the lord and lady

rounded towers

high stone walls

arrow-loop – narrow slits where people fired bows and arrows, and threw spears and rocks

drawbridge which could be raised

portcullis (armoured gate)

moat

barracks for soldiers

kitchen

Many castles were surrounded by a moat of water. This made it very hard for enemies to capture the castle.

People could defend themselves for a long time within a castle if they had water and a store of food.

When guns and gunpowder were invented in the thirteenth century, castles became very hard to defend.

CAT

SEE ALSO • Animal • Mammal • Pet

A cat is a mammal. Cats belong to the same family as tigers, lions, leopards, panthers and jaguars. Unlike these wild cats, most cats are tame.

PARTS OF A CAT

tail to help keep balance when jumping

fur

ears for supersensitive hearing

keen eyes for hunting

Each toe has a claw which can be drawn into a sheath.

sensitive whiskers

5 toes on back feet

4 toes on front feet

Height: 20 to 25 centimetres   **Weight:** 4 to 8 kilograms

◄ The ancient Egyptians worshipped the cat as a god.

FOOD

Cats are flesh-eaters (carnivores).

small animals

A PET CAT

A cat needs:
- a warm, dry place to sleep
- fresh drinking water every day
- fresh food every day
- brushing every day
- loving care
- space to exercise.

INTERESTING FACT

Cats can see better in dim light than humans can.

CATS AS HUNTERS

Cats are good hunters. They can be helpful by catching mice. They can also be a danger to wildlife. Cats should be kept in at night.

HOW CATS LIVE

- A female cat chooses a secret, dark place to have her kittens.
- Usually four to five kittens are born in a litter.
- A mother cat feeds her kittens with milk for eight weeks.
- A kitten's eyes do not open for eight to ten days. Bright light could injure the kitten's eyes.
- Most cats live for about 14 years.

KINDS OF CATS

There are many different kinds of cats. They are divided into long-haired cats and short-haired cats.

Short-haired cats
Burmese cat

Siamese cat

Russian Blue

Long-haired cats
Persian cat

Turkish angora cat

CATTLE

SEE ALSO • Farming • Food • Ungulates • Yak

Cattle are grazing farm animals. They belong to the ox family. Cattle are found in most places of the world. There are two main kinds of farm cattle: dairy and beef cattle.

PARTS OF BEEF CATTLE

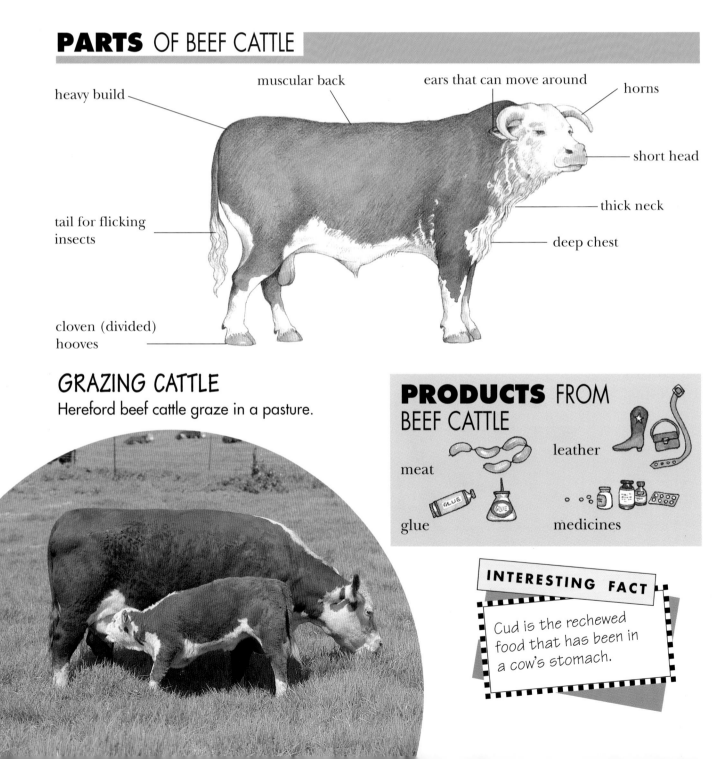

heavy build

muscular back

ears that can move around

horns

short head

thick neck

deep chest

tail for flicking insects

cloven (divided) hooves

GRAZING CATTLE

Hereford beef cattle graze in a pasture.

PRODUCTS FROM BEEF CATTLE

meat

leather

glue

medicines

INTERESTING FACT

Cud is the rechewed food that has been in a cow's stomach.

PARTS OF DAIRY CATTLE

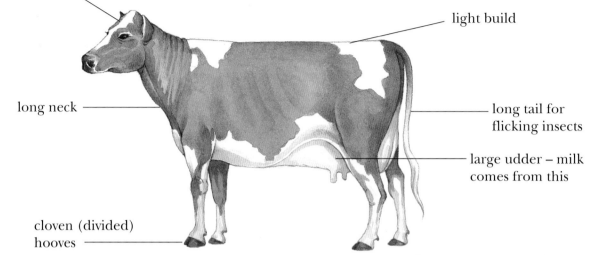

ears which move to hear sounds

light build

long neck

long tail for flicking insects

large udder – milk comes from this

cloven (divided) hooves

DAIRY COWS ▶

Dairy cows produce milk. They are milked in a milking shed. Milk is obtained from the udder by squeezing the teats. Cows can be milked by hand or by machine.

PRODUCTS FROM DAIRY CATTLE

milk   cheese   yoghurt   butter   ice cream

FOOD

Cattle are plant-eaters (herbivores).

hay

corn

grass

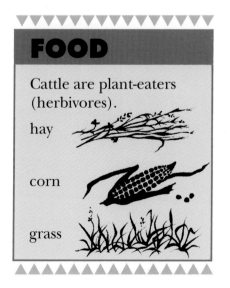

FOUR STOMACHS

A cow has four parts to its stomach. When a cow grazes, the grass is stored in one part of its stomach. Later, the cow brings up the grass to rechew it. When the rechewed grass is swallowed, it passes to another part of the stomach. This helps the cow to digest its food.

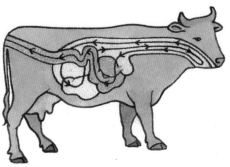

CAVE

SEE ALSO • Bat • House • Rocks • Volcano

A cave is a natural hole. Caves are dark, damp places. Some caves are big enough to shelter a person or an animal. Other caves are a large network of caves linked together.

KINDS OF CAVES

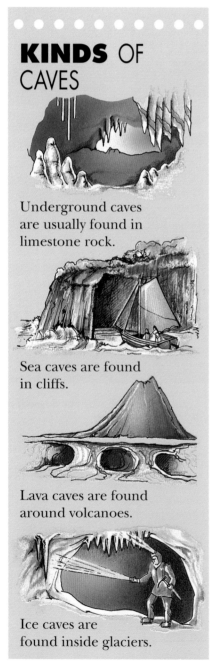

Underground caves are usually found in limestone rock.

Sea caves are found in cliffs.

Lava caves are found around volcanoes.

Ice caves are found inside glaciers.

HISTORY

Thousands of years ago, people used caves as their homes. Caves provided shelter from the weather and protection from wild animals. Ancient rock paintings, and pieces of tools and weapons have been found in caves.

FAMOUS CAVES

Some caves are famous because of their ancient paintings. Other caves have beautiful formations of stalactites and stalagmites. The Waitomo Caves in New Zealand have glow-worms on their roofs.

HOW A LIMESTONE CAVE IS MADE

- Water slowly dissolves limestone rock. It seeps through cracks in the rock.
- Over thousands of years, the acid in the water slowly makes caves and passages.
- Water flows in to make an underground stream. It feeds an underground river.

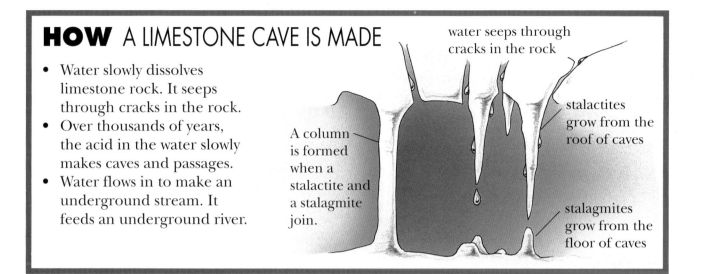

water seeps through cracks in the rock

stalactites grow from the roof of caves

A column is formed when a stalactite and a stalagmite join.

stalagmites grow from the floor of caves

STALACTITES AND STALAGMITES

Stalactites and stalagmites are like stone icicles. They are found inside limestone caves. They are formed from drops of water that contain a mineral called calcite. When the water dries, a tiny bit of calcite is left behind. Over thousands of years, the calcite builds up to form stalactites and stalagmites.

SEA CAVES ▶

Caves along the coast are formed by waves pounding on the rocks.

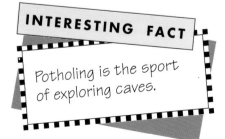

INTERESTING FACT

Potholing is the sport of exploring caves.

CIRCUS

SEE ALSO • Drama • Ears • Gymnastics

A circus is a show that travels from town to town.
Some big circuses go on tour to different countries.
A circus has clowns, acrobats, trapeze artists and
performing animals.

KINDS OF CLOWNS

Clowns make people laugh.

Auguste

Auguste clowns wear
baggy clothes and have a
round, red nose.

Joey

The Joey clown has a
white face.

THE BIG TOP

Circus people live in caravans. A circus can be
moved from town to town by trucks or train.
The circus is performed in a big tent. The big
top supports the lighting. It also supports the
rigging for trapeze acts. People sit around the
circus ring to watch the acts. The ringmaster
introduces the circus acts and keeps the
performance running smoothly.

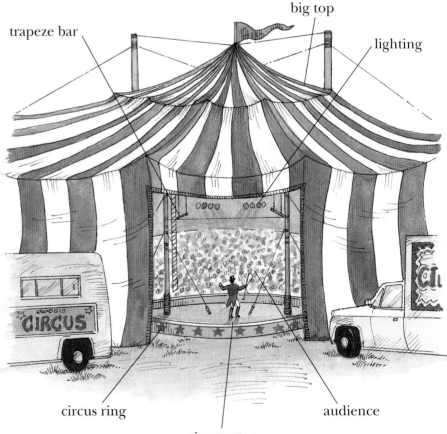

trapeze bar

big top

lighting

circus ring

ringmaster

audience

PERFORMING ANIMALS

Animals can be trained to perform tricks. Many people think it is cruel to treat animals in this way. Some circuses only have human performers.

The circus we know today started in the eighteenth century.

TRAPEZE ▶ ARTISTS

Trapeze artists perform on a tightrope and on swings high in the air.

CIRCUS MUSIC ▲

Music is specially written for circus performances.

ACROBATS AND JUGGLERS

Acrobats jump and turn somersaults. Jugglers throw things in the air. You need good balance, coordination and lots of practice to be a successful acrobat or juggler.

CLOCK

SEE ALSO
• Calendar • Days of the Week
• Months of the Year • Quartz

A clock is an instrument for measuring time.
A clock measures hours, minutes and seconds.

PARTS OF A CLOCK

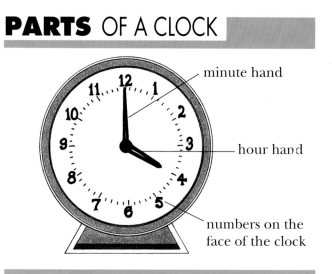

minute hand

hour hand

numbers on the
face of the clock

There are 60 seconds in 1 minute,
60 minutes in 1 hour and 24 hours
in a day.

HISTORY

Long ago, people measured
time by shadows. They put
a stick in the ground and
watched its shadow move
with the Sun.

HOW A CLOCK WORKS

Inside a clock there are a lot of small
wheels. Springs unwind and make the
wheels go round.
• The hour hand is attached to a wheel
  that goes around twice a day.
• The minute hand is attached to a
  wheel that goes around once an hour.

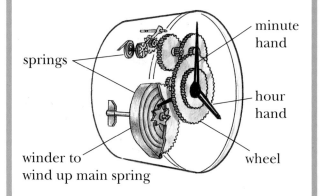

springs

minute
hand

hour
hand

winder to
wind up main spring

wheel

All clocks need power to work. Power
can come from a spring, weights,
electricity or batteries.

DIGITAL WATCH

Digital watches show the time by changing
numbers. They work by using electricity from
a tiny battery.

A clock stands on
its own. A watch
is a small clock
which is put
around the wrist.

CLOTHES

Clothes protect us from heat, cold, rain, snow and dust. People choose clothes to suit the weather and the way they live.

The material that clothes are made from is called fabric. Lightweight fabrics are usually worn when the weather is hot. Heavier fabrics such as wool are used to make winter clothes.

SEE ALSO
• Cotton • Firefighters
• Heat • Heritage

NATIONAL DRESS

For special occasions, some people like to wear the costume of their area.

UNIFORMS

Some uniforms show a person's work. Other uniforms show that a person is part of a group.

◀ PROTECTIVE CLOTHING

Protective clothing helps to keep people such as firefighters safe.

HISTORY

Clothes keep changing over the years. We can find out about the clothes people wore long ago from paintings, statues, diaries and photographs. Clothes that look fancy to us today were once everyday clothing.

CLOUD

SEE ALSO
• Rain • Water • Weather

A cloud is a mass of tiny water drops or ice crystals. Clouds float in the air. There are different clouds in different levels of the sky.

DIFFERENT KINDS OF CLOUDS

There are many different kinds of clouds. The three main kinds are cirrus, cumulus and stratus. These names are combined to describe the other kinds of clouds.

- Cirrus clouds are wispy clouds. These clouds signal that rain is coming. They are the highest in the sky.

- Cumulus clouds are fluffy heaps of clouds. Small cumulus clouds can signal that fine weather is on the way. When these clouds are bigger or darker, they signal that snow or rain is on the way.

- Stratus clouds are sheets of cloud across the sky. They are the lowest in the sky. These clouds often bring rain.

HOW CLOUDS ARE MADE

1. Water on the Earth turns into water vapour and rises into the air.
2. As the air cools, water vapour is changed into drops of water which form clouds.
3. When the air can no longer hold the water drops, they fall as rain.

rain

cloud

water vapour

INTERESTING FACT

Clouds keep the Earth warm at night. They stop heat escaping into space.

◄ Sometimes, there may be more than two or three different kinds of clouds at different levels of the sky at one time.

COAL

SEE ALSO • Conservation • Electricity • Fossil • Mining

Coal is soft, black or brown rock. It is mostly made of carbon. Coal is used as a fuel. It is burned at power stations to make electricity. It is also used to make coal gas and coke, which are other important fuels.

HOW COAL IS MADE

1. Coal is made from the remains of huge trees and other plants.

2. Over many years, as plants died, their remains built up in layers and sank into the ground.

3. Millions of years passed. The weight of the Earth pressing down changed the dead plant material into coal.

COAL MINING

Coal is mined from deep under the ground.

Coal is a fossil fuel. Fossil fuels are formed from the remains of plants and animals that lived on Earth millions of years ago. Once used, fossil fuels cannot be replaced.

COAL PRODUCTS

plastics

medicines

dyes

explosives

chemicals

fuel

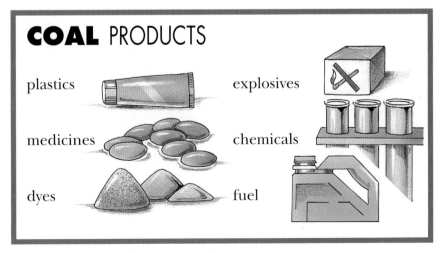

COLOUR

SEE ALSO
• Camouflage • Light
• Painting • Rainbow

Colour is all around us. Everything in the world has colour. White light is a mixture of all colours. It can be broken up into separate colours.

PRIMARY COLOURS

Red, blue and yellow are primary colours. Primary colours are mixed to make secondary colours.

blue + red = violet

Violet is a secondary colour.

red + yellow = orange

Orange is a secondary colour.

yellow + blue = green

Green is a secondary colour.

MIXING COLOURS

All other colours can be mixed from these six colours – red, blue, yellow, violet, orange and green.

COLOUR IN EVERYDAY LIFE

Colour is used in everyday life as signals. Traffic lights tell us when to stop and go.

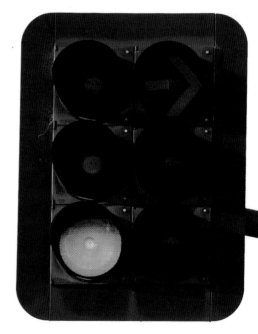

COLOUR-BLINDNESS

Colour-blindness is when you cannot see some colours, such as red and green.

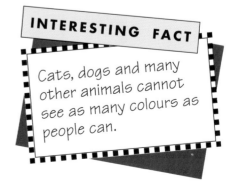

INTERESTING FACT

Cats, dogs and many other animals cannot see as many colours as people can.

COMPOST

SEE ALSO • Earthworm • Garden • Recycling

Compost is decayed plant and animal matter.
It is like a rich black or brown crumbly soil.
It is made from food scraps and garden cuttings.

HOW TO MAKE COMPOST

1. You can make compost in a large container or in a heap.

2. Insects, worms, bacteria and fungi feed on the dead matter. They break it down into smaller pieces.

3. The decayed plant and animal matter provides growing plants with food (nutrients). Plants need nutrients to grow.

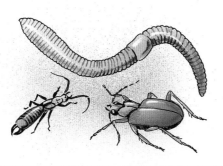

A GARDEN COMPOST BIN

Compost bins are containers to collect kitchen scraps and garden rubbish so that it can decay. Once decayed, the compost can be used to feed the soil.

LANDFILL SITES

Most household rubbish is buried in landfill sites. Composting reduces the amount of rubbish that is sent to landfill sites.

Earthworms help to break down kitchen and garden rubbish into nutrients for the soil. ▲

COMPUTER

SEE ALSO
• Bank • Hospital • Printing
• School • Weather

A computer is an electronic machine. Computers cannot think. They can be given instructions and information to carry out many tasks. A computer works very quickly. It can multiply 4763 by 7915 in a split second.

PARTS OF A COMPUTER

Output
This is where results are produced so we can use them. Visual display units, printers, voice and sound are for communication between you and the computer.

Central processing unit (CPU)
This is the heart of the computer. Information is processed here.

Memory
Information and instructions are stored here.

Input
The keyboard and mouse are for communication between you and the computer.

- **Data** is information put into the computer.
- A **program** is a set of instructions.
- Data and programs are called **software**.
- Computers store data and programs on **RAM** and **ROM** chips in the central processing unit (CPU).
- Some devices which are used to put information into the computer are a joystick, a lightpen, a 'mouse' and a keyboard. You can use your voice to put information into some computers. Information can be shared and used all over the world.

Computers are used in almost every part of our lives.

In factories, computers can control machines.

Computers calculate the best route for an aeroplane flight.

In banks, computers are used to check and calculate money.

In hospitals, computers can keep records.

Computers can help make real-life images.

Pilots can learn to fly aeroplanes without leaving the ground by using a computer.

Computers are useful tools for learning. ▶

◀ Computers can make accurate weather forecasts from weather reports.

ELECTRONIC MAIL

People can send messages to each other through their computer using a modem, which is connected to the telephone system.

Interactive programs can make computer games exciting.
▼

CONSERVATION

SEE ALSO • Ecology • Endangered Species • Pollution • Recycling

Conservation is looking after and caring for the environment. The environment includes natural resources such as water, soil, minerals, forests and wildlife.

We need to think and act together to protect and conserve our world. People have to:
- stop polluting rivers and oceans
- save forests
- conserve fossil fuels such as coal, gas and oil
- keep the air clean
- stop animals and plants from becoming extinct.

CLEAN AIR AND CLEAN WATER

All life on Earth needs clean air to breathe and clean water to drink.

ENERGY

Most of our energy on Earth comes from oil ▶ products, coal and natural gas. These are limited resources. Once they are used, they cannot be replaced. We need to conserve energy to make these resources last longer.

◀ Scientists have developed solar cells to give us power. Solar cells use the Sun's energy. Solar power will never run out, and it is non-polluting.

FOOD CHAIN

All living things need food. Each plant or animal is food for another living thing. Together, they form a food chain. Every link is vital, even tiny insects. If you remove just one link, the chain can be broken. This affects the rest of the food chain.

Sun → tree → caterpillar → bird

◀ HABITAT

To save and protect most animals, the place where they live (habitat) must be saved and protected.

CONTINENT

SEE ALSO
• Antarctica • Earth
• Ocean

A continent is a large area of land. There are seven continents on Earth – Europe, Asia, North America, South America, Africa, Australia and Antarctica.

North America

Atlantic Ocean

Pacific Ocean

South America

North America is a large continent with ten different countries. It has tall mountains, flat plains and hot deserts as well as glaciers.

South America is a large continent which has many countries. It has the largest rain forest in the world, the Amazon.

North

West ← → East

South

INTERESTING FACT

About 250 million years ago, all the continents on Earth were joined together.

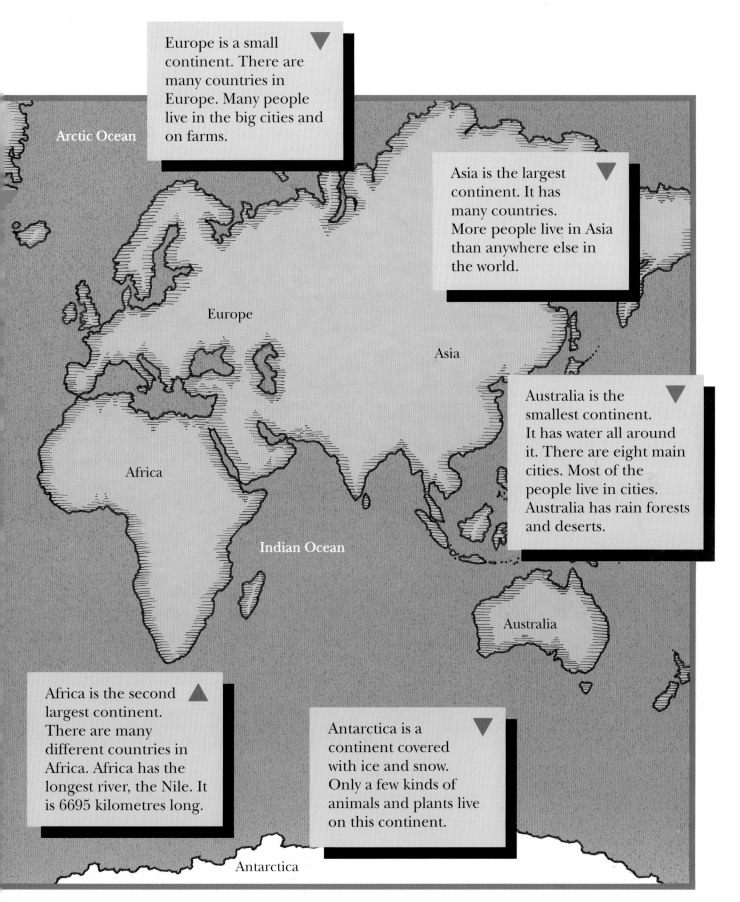

Arctic Ocean

Europe is a small
continent. There are
many countries in
Europe. Many people
live in the big cities and
on farms.

Asia is the largest
continent. It has
many countries.
More people live in Asia
than anywhere else in
the world.

Europe

Asia

Australia is the
smallest continent.
It has water all around
it. There are eight main
cities. Most of the
people live in cities.
Australia has rain forests
and deserts.

Africa

Indian Ocean

Australia

Africa is the second
largest continent.
There are many
different countries in
Africa. Africa has the
longest river, the Nile. It
is 6695 kilometres long.

Antarctica is a
continent covered
with ice and snow.
Only a few kinds of
animals and plants live
on this continent.

Antarctica

CORAL

SEE ALSO
• Animal • Invertebrate
• Island • Jellyfish

Coral is found in warm seas. Each coral is made up of tiny animals called coral polyps. Jellyfish and sea anemones belong to the same group of animals. Corals can be many different shapes, sizes and colours.

PARTS OF A CORAL POLYP

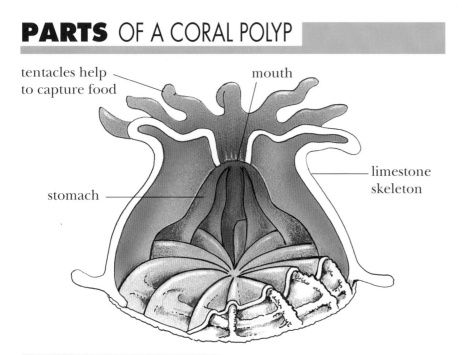

tentacles help to capture food

mouth

stomach

limestone skeleton

A coral polyp has a simple body. It builds a limestone, cup-shaped skeleton around itself. Most polyps live in small or large groups called colonies. They spend the day hiding in their skeletons. They come out at night to feed.

FOOD

plankton

CORAL POLYPS

Many corals are beautiful colours under the water. They may be bright green, orange, pink, purple or yellow. The shape of the coral depends on the tiny polyps that build it.

KINDS OF CORAL

There are two kinds of coral – hard coral and soft coral.

- Hard coral has a hard, protective skeleton. A hard coral has six feathery tentacles around its mouth.

- Soft coral does not have a hard, protective skeleton. A soft coral has eight feathery tentacles around its mouth.

CORAL REEFS

A coral reef is made from the limestone skeletons of coral. When coral polyps die, their skeletons add to the reef bed. Coral reefs provide shelter and homes for many sea animals.

HOW A CORAL ATOLL IS MADE

A coral atoll is ring-shaped.

1. Some coral grows in warm waters around an island.

2. The coral reef grows as the island sinks.

3. The island disappears leaving a ring of coral.

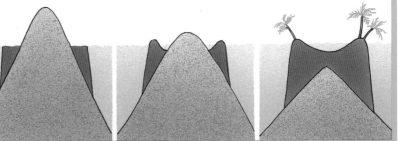

SEA ANEMONES ▶

Sea anemones provide a home for clown fish.

COTTON

SEE ALSO • Clothing • Farming • Plant

Cotton is a plant that is used to make cloth.
Cotton cloth is used to make clothes.

THE COTTON PLANT

The cotton plant grows green fruits called bolls. When the bolls are ripe, they split open. Inside the boll are large, white tufts of fibre around the seed. The ripe bolls are picked.

PICKING COTTON

Cotton can be picked by hand and by machines.

WHERE COTTON GROWS

● USA
■ Russia
◆ India
★ Brazil
▲ China
▼ Egypt
✖ Australia

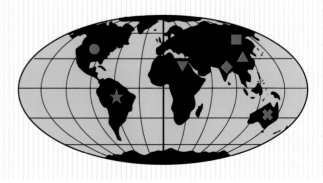

HOW COTTON CLOTH IS MADE

1. Cotton fibres are cleaned to remove seeds.

2. Cotton fibres are spun into yarn.

3. The yarn is woven into cloth.

PRODUCTS

Some products are made from the white fibre of cotton. Some products are made from the cotton seed.

clothes

bandages

cotton wool

paper

paint

rugs

towels

sheets

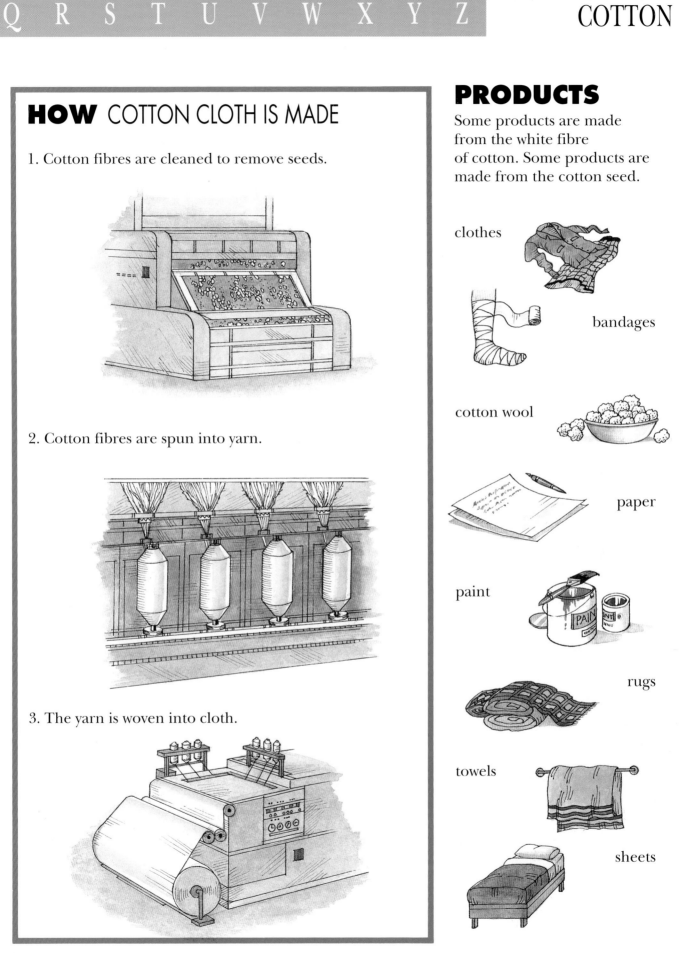

CRAB

SEE ALSO
• Animal • Invertebrate
• Seashore Life

A crab is an animal with a hard skeleton outside its body.
It has five pairs of legs. Many crabs walk sideways.
Crabs can live in fresh water or sea water.
Some crabs live on land.

PARTS OF A CRAB

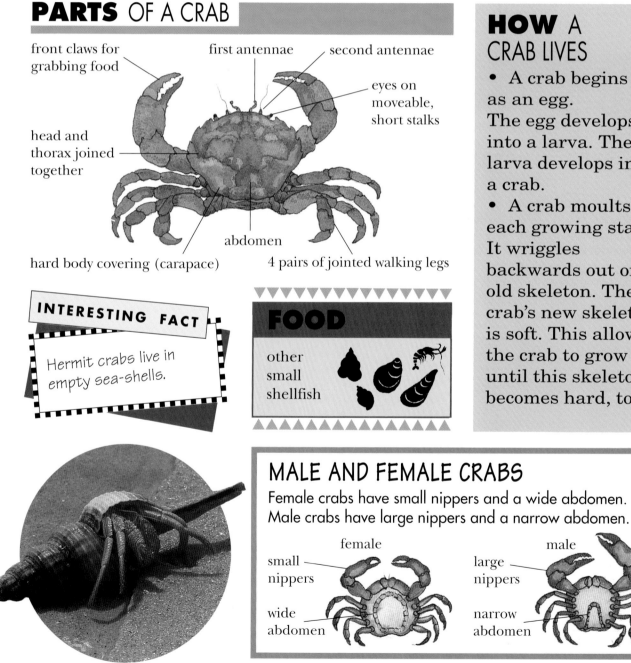

front claws for grabbing food

first antennae

second antennae

eyes on moveable, short stalks

head and thorax joined together

abdomen

hard body covering (carapace)

4 pairs of jointed walking legs

HOW A CRAB LIVES

• A crab begins life as an egg.
The egg develops into a larva. The larva develops into a crab.
• A crab moults at each growing stage. It wriggles backwards out of its old skeleton. The crab's new skeleton is soft. This allows the crab to grow until this skeleton becomes hard, too.

INTERESTING FACT

Hermit crabs live in empty sea-shells.

FOOD

other small shellfish

MALE AND FEMALE CRABS

Female crabs have small nippers and a wide abdomen.
Male crabs have large nippers and a narrow abdomen.

female

small nippers

wide abdomen

male

large nippers

narrow abdomen

CRICKET

SEE ALSO • Baseball • Tennis

Cricket is a game played with a bat, a ball and wickets. You need two teams to play cricket. Each team has 11 players. One team bats, while the other team bowls and fields. It can be played by boys and girls.

THE CRICKET FIELD

The bowler bowls the ball to the batsman.

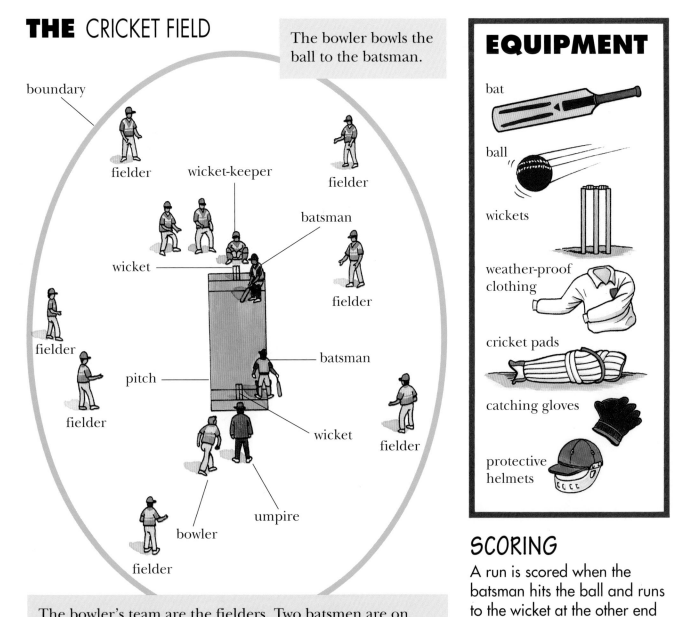

boundary

fielder

wicket-keeper

fielder

batsman

wicket

fielder

fielder

batsman

pitch

wicket

fielder

fielder

umpire

bowler

fielder

The bowler's team are the fielders. Two batsmen are on the field at the same time. Both of them run when the ball is hit, and they may change places with one another.

EQUIPMENT

bat

ball

wickets

weather-proof clothing

cricket pads

catching gloves

protective helmets

SCORING

A run is scored when the batsman hits the ball and runs to the wicket at the other end of the pitch. The batting team is out when ten batsmen have been hit out.

CYCLONE

SEE ALSO • Air • Atmosphere • Satellite • Weather • Wind

A cyclone is a violent tropical storm. Cyclones begin over an ocean. Strong winds begin to spiral around the eye of the storm, which becomes the centre of the cyclone.

HOW CYCLONES FORM

1. Warm air rises quickly.
2. Cold air is sucked in to replace warm air.
3. Winds spiral outwards.
4. The centre remains calm.

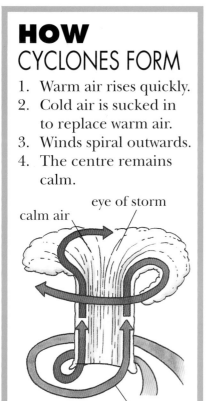

calm air

eye of storm

spiralling winds

SATELLITE TRACKING STATION

Satellites can be used to watch cyclones. Meteorologists use satellite tracking information to learn about the movement of cyclones. People can then be moved to safety.

◀ CYCLONE DAMAGE

Cyclones can cause great damage to houses, trees, roads and crops.

INTERESTING FACT

A cyclone is called a typhoon in Asia.
A cyclone is called a hurricane in the USA.

DAM

SEE ALSO • Bridge • Electricity • Flood • Irrigation • River • Rodents

A dam is a barrier which is built across a river to stop it flowing. A huge lake forms behind the dam. This is a reservoir.

KINDS OF DAMS

Concrete dams

• Arch dam
Tall, curved walls make these dams strong.

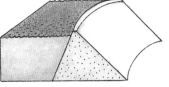

• Gravity dam
The vast weight of the walls stops them giving way.

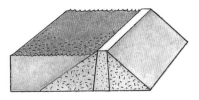

Embankment dams
Embankment dams have a huge barrier made of earth and rock.

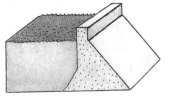

A RESERVOIR ▲

• A reservoir stores huge amounts of water. The water is used to water farms when the rainfall is low or in times of drought.
• The water is sent in pipes to cities and towns. People use it for drinking, washing and cooking.
• A dam can contain hydro-electric power stations. Water from reservoirs is used to turn generators that make electricity.

BEAVERS ▶

Beavers make a dam in a river or a stream. They use sticks, stone and mud. A lake forms behind the dam. This is where beavers make their home, which is called a lodge.

DANCING

SEE ALSO • Ballet • Festival • Gymnastics • Music

Dancing is moving your body to music.
You can dance by yourself or with another person.
There are many kinds of dancing.

Some dancing is a story set to music. The story is told through the movement of the dancer's body. In some countries, dancing is a part of religious ceremonies.

FOLK DANCING ▼

Folk dances are very old dances. They often belong to a group of people or come from a particular region.

◄ BALLROOM DANCING

Two people dance together for ballroom dancing. Each dance has its own dancing steps and movements.

BALINESE ▶ DANCERS

Balinese dancers use their hands, eyes, feet and arms to tell the story of their dance.

NATIVE AMERICANS

Native Americans dance to celebrate changes in nature, such as the coming of spring.

DAYS OF THE WEEK

| SEE ALSO | • Calendar • Clock • Months of the Year |

A day is the time it takes for the Earth to spin around once on its axis.

The side of the Earth which faces the Sun is in daylight. As the Earth keeps spinning away from the Sun, it becomes dark. Night begins. When it spins back to the Sun again, another day begins.

Weeks were invented by people. Long ago, people wanted a time longer than a day and shorter than a month. They decided to have a week of seven days.

Wednesday
The fourth day of the week was named Woden's day after Woden, a very wise god. We call it Wednesday.

Sunday
Long ago, people worshipped the Sun. They called the first day of the week Sun's Day. We call it Sunday.

Thursday
The fifth day of the week was named Thor's day after Thor, the Norse god of thunder. We call it Thursday.

Monday
Long ago, people thought of the second day of the week as the Moon's Day. We call it Monday.

Friday
The sixth day of the week was named Freya's day after Freya, the wife of the chief of gods. We call it Friday.

Tuesday
The third day of the week was named Tiw's day after Tiw, an Anglo-Saxon god of war. We call it Tuesday.

Saturday
The seventh day of the week was named Saturn's day after the planet Saturn. We call it Saturday.

DEER

SEE ALSO
• Animal • Arctic • Mammal
• Ungulates

A deer is a mammal. It is a hoofed animal. Deer can run very fast.

PARTS OF A MALE WHITE-TAILED DEER

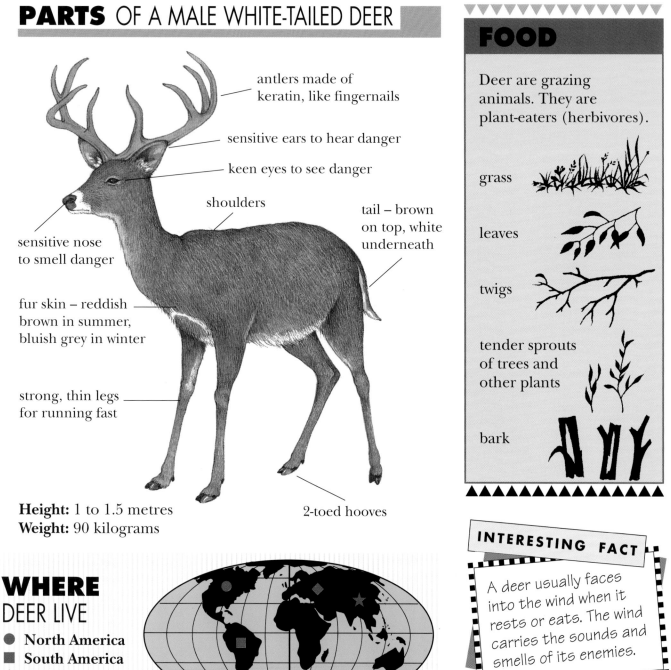

antlers made of keratin, like fingernails

sensitive ears to hear danger

keen eyes to see danger

shoulders

tail – brown on top, white underneath

sensitive nose to smell danger

fur skin – reddish brown in summer, bluish grey in winter

strong, thin legs for running fast

Height: 1 to 1.5 metres
Weight: 90 kilograms

2-toed hooves

FOOD

Deer are grazing animals. They are plant-eaters (herbivores).

grass

leaves

twigs

tender sprouts of trees and other plants

bark

WHERE DEER LIVE

● **North America**
■ **South America**
◆ **Europe**
★ **Asia**

INTERESTING FACT

A deer usually faces into the wind when it rests or eats. The wind carries the sounds and smells of its enemies.

HOW DEER LIVE

- Most deer live in groups called herds. Deer defend their group against other herds.
- During autumn, male deer fight with each other to win a group of female deer. The biggest and strongest deer usually win.
- Young deer are called fawns. Fawns stay hidden after they are born until they can walk well enough to follow their mother. They stay with their mother for more than one year.

INTERESTING FACT

Reindeer are the only deer where both males and females have antlers. Usually, only male deer have antlers.

REINDEER ▼

The Lapps of Northern Finland keep herds of reindeer. Reindeer can be tamed and used to pull sledges.

DEER FARMS

Some deer are kept as farm animals. Deer are farmed to provide meat and leather.

DEER SIZES

- Moose are the largest deer. A moose is 2.3 metres tall at its shoulders. It weighs 800 kilograms.
- The smallest deer is the Pudu which lives in Chile. It is only 33 centimetres tall and weighs 8 kilograms.

ANTLERS

Deer shed their antlers each year and grow a new pair. The new antlers begin as stumps covered with a layer of soft, hairy skin and are fully grown in a year.

DESERT

SEE ALSO • Camel • Continent • Earth • Plant

A desert is a dry place. Deserts can be hot or cold, but they are always dry. Very little rain falls in a desert. About one-fifth of the Earth's land surface is desert.

Some deserts can get very hot in the daytime, but very cold at night. At night, the land loses its heat quickly.

DESERTS OF THE WORLD

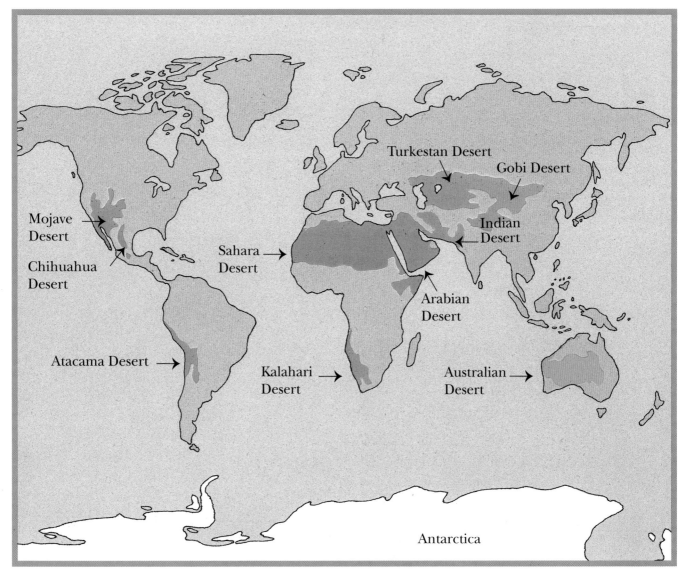

Mojave Desert

Chihuahua Desert

Atacama Desert

Turkestan Desert

Gobi Desert

Indian Desert

Sahara Desert

Arabian Desert

Kalahari Desert

Australian Desert

Antarctica

Most deserts are in the middle of continents.
Most winds are dry by the time they reach the
middle of large continents.

SAND DUNES ▼

The wind sweeps sand into
great hills called sand dunes.

OASIS ▲

An oasis is a place in the
desert where there is a
spring or well of water.
People can live in an oasis
and grow crops.

NOMADS ▼

Some people who live in the desert are called nomads.
They move around the desert driving their animals from one
grazing place to another.

DESERT
ANIMALS AND PLANTS

Many animals and
plants can survive
in the desert. Many
desert animals
shelter by day. They
come out at night
when it is cooler.
They need little
water to survive.

A cactus is a desert plant. It
stores water in its fleshy stem.
The cactus's spines prevent
animals eating it for its water.

Gerbils live in the deserts of
South East Asia and Africa.
They need little water, and
feed on seeds and leaves.

The camel is a desert animal.
It stores food in its hump and
can go without water for
many days.

DIGESTION

SEE ALSO • Blood • Food • Human Body • Vitamins

Digestion is the way food is broken down in the body. Food provides energy for your body. Your body needs energy to grow.

THE DIGESTIVE SYSTEM

1. Food is chewed into small pieces and mixed with saliva.

2. In the stomach, food is mixed with digestive juices. It is churned into a soft paste.

3. Food passes to the small intestine. It is broken down with bile from the liver and juice from the pancreas.

4. Fluid from the food passes through the wall of the small intestine into the blood. Food travels to all parts of the body in the blood.

5. Waste passes into the large intestine. It leaves the body as faeces.

On its journey through the body, food is broken down by chemicals called enzymes. Enzymes turn the food into substances the body needs.

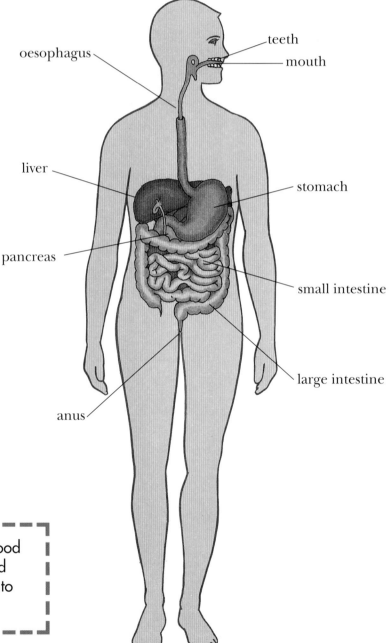

oesophagus

teeth

mouth

liver

stomach

pancreas

small intestine

large intestine

anus

YOUR DIGESTION TIMETABLE

Digestion is the process of breaking down food. It starts as soon as you put food into your mouth. The mouth, oesophagus, stomach and intestines are part of the digestive system.

First day

12.30 am	Stomach is empty.
8 am	Breakfast is eaten.
	Food enters stomach after four to six seconds.
4 pm	Food has passed through small intestine.

Second day

| 8 am | Waste from food eaten the day before is ready to leave the large intestine. |

Third day

| 8 am | 48 hours after the first meal, the last of the waste is ready to leave the large intestine. |

MOUTH

- Teeth chew food into pulp.
- The tongue tastes the food.
- Salivary glands produce saliva which is mixed with the food. This makes it easy to swallow.

OESOPHAGUS

- Food is pushed into the stomach.

STOMACH

- The stomach is like a J-shaped bag.
- The food moves into the intestine.

SMALL INTESTINE

- The small intestine is a long coiled tube about 6.5 metres long.

LARGE INTESTINE

- The large intestine is shorter than the small intestine. It is about 1.5 metres long, but three times as wide.

ANUS

- Waste products leave the body as faeces.

◀ Food is necessary for our bodies. Most people enjoy eating. It is fun to join together and enjoy special meals.

DINOSAUR

SEE ALSO • Fossil • Heritage • Reptiles

A dinosaur is an animal that lived millions of years ago, before people lived on Earth. Dinosaur means 'terrible lizard'. Dinosaurs lived on Earth for nearly 150 million years. They disappeared from Earth 65 million years ago.

DINOSAUR EGGS

Like most reptiles and birds, dinosaurs laid hard-shelled eggs on land.

FOSSILS

- We know what dinosaurs looked like from bones and teeth which have been found in rocks.
- We know how dinosaurs moved by the footprints and tracks they left in mud which turned to rock.

- The shape and arrangement of their jaws and teeth tell us what they ate.

INTERESTING FACT

The nearest living reptile relative of dinosaurs are crocodiles.

WHY DID DINOSAURS DIE?

Scientists are unsure why dinosaurs died out.
- It could have been because the climate became colder. Dinosaurs would not have been able to keep warm or find food.
- Some scientists think that there was a great disaster on Earth that caused the dinosaurs to become extinct.

KINDS OF DINOSAURS

Brontosaurus was one of the giant dinosaurs. It had a heavy body, a long neck and a long tail. It was one of the largest land animals ever to have lived.

Length: 21 metres

Diplodocus was the longest ever land animal. It had a tiny head, a long neck and a long tail like a whip. Its strong, straight legs supported its body.

Length: 27 metres

Stegosaurus was a plant-eating dinosaur. It fed on ground plants. This dinosaur was heavily armoured with a row of plates down its back. It could defend itself with a swish of its pronged tail.

Length: up to 9 metres

Allosaurus was a meat-eating dinosaur. It had sharp teeth and claws which it used to tear apart its food. It weighed more than an elephant.

Length: 11 metres

Tyrannosaurus was one of the biggest meat-eating dinosaurs. A person would just reach to its knee. It had strong jaws lined with large, sharp teeth. A single tooth would be up to 18 centimetres long.
Size: 15 metres long and 6 metres high

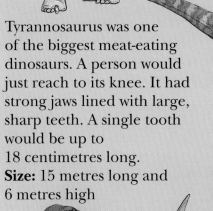

Triceratops had three sharp horns – one on its nose and two long ones above its eyes. Triceratops was very large, but it could move quickly to escape its enemies.

Length: 9 metres

Brachiosaurus was the tallest dinosaur. It was as tall as a three-storey building. It could eat the highest branches of tall trees.

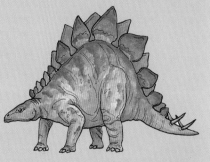

Length: 23 metres

DOCTOR

SEE ALSO • Ambulance • Drug • Hospital • X-ray

A doctor helps sick people to get well and stay healthy.
Doctors try to find out what caused an illness.
Then, they try to cure it.

MEDICAL INSTRUMENTS

Doctors use medical instruments to find out why people are sick.

Doctors use a blood-pressure cuff to check blood pressure.

Doctors use a stethoscope to listen to the heart and lungs and other sounds inside the body.

Doctors use an ophthalmoscope to examine the eyes.

Doctors use an otoscope to examine the ears.

Doctors use a thermometer to check a patient's temperature.

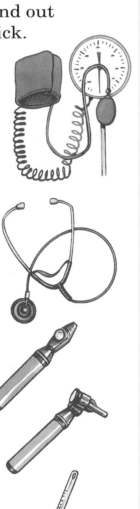

X-RAYS

X-ray machines take photographs of the inside of your body. Doctors look at the X-ray to find out if you are injured.

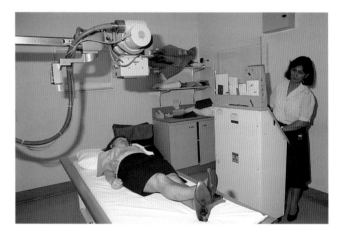

VACCINATION

Doctors help prevent diseases. They give vaccinations to guard against diseases such as polio and measles.

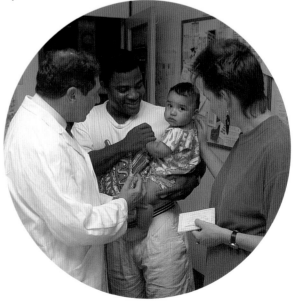

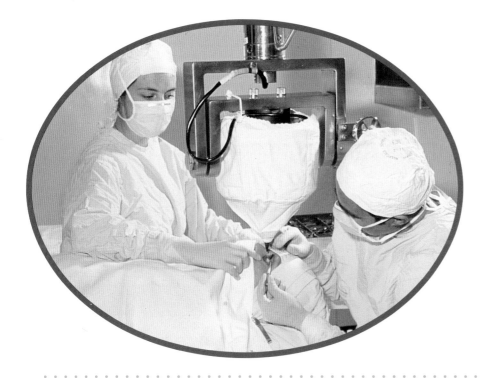

OPERATIONS

Sometimes, people need an operation to fix parts of the body. Operations are performed in a hospital in an operating theatre. Doctors work with a surgical team to perform operations.

MEDICINE

Doctors use many different kinds of drugs such as penicillin to cure disease.

DENTIST

A dentist is a doctor who looks after the teeth and mouth.
A dentist's most important work is to prevent disease and decay of the teeth or mouth. You need to visit a dentist regularly for a check-up to keep your teeth in good condition.

FILLING TEETH ▶

If a dentist finds decay in a tooth, he or she will drill out the decayed bit. This leaves a hole which is filled.
An injection of a local anaesthetic into the gum near the tooth makes the tooth's nerves numb. This stops any pain.

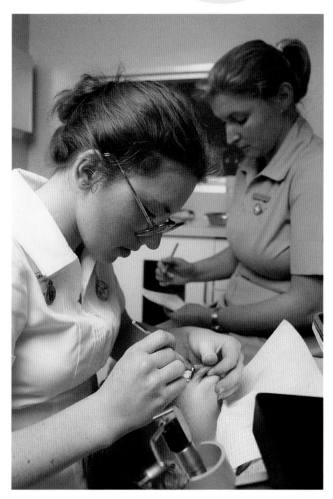

DOG

SEE ALSO • Animal • Mammal • Pet • Wolf

A dog is a mammal. Dogs are popular pets. Many dogs help people and are working animals. Dogs belong to the same family as wolves, coyotes, jackals and dingoes.

PARTS OF A DOG

eyes

ears for listening well

nose for smelling

strong jaws and teeth

tail

front legs

back legs

5 claws on front paws

4 claws on back paws

WORKING DOGS

Many dogs are trained for special work to help people. They learn to obey commands.

INTERESTING FACT

The tallest dog in the world is an Irish wolfhound. It is 1.5 metres tall. The smallest dog is the chihuahua. It is smaller than a pigeon.

FOOD

Dogs are meat-eating animals (carnivores).

HOW DOGS LIVE

- A female dog gives birth to 1 to 12 puppies at a time.
- A puppy is born with its eyes closed. A puppy's eyes open after 10 to 14 days.
- The mother feeds the puppies with her milk until they are four to five weeks old.
- At eight months to two years, a dog is fully grown.
- A dog lives for 12 to 14 years.

PET DOGS

A dog needs:
- warm, dry shelter
- a place to sleep
- fresh food every day
- fresh drinking water every day
- exercise every day
- brushing every day to clean its fur and keep it free from insects
- loving care.

KINDS OF DOGS

There are many different kinds of dogs.

Sporting dogs

terrier
hound
gun dog

Working dogs

collie
Saint Bernard
husky

Toy dogs

Pekingese
Maltese
chihuahua

Non-sporting dogs

Dalmatian
bulldog
poodle

DOLL

SEE ALSO • Festival • Hobby • Toy

A doll is a toy shaped like a person. All over the world, children play with dolls in all shapes and sizes. Some dolls take a long time to make. Other dolls are made from simple materials.

MODERN DOLLS

New kinds of dolls are being made all the time.

FESTIVALS AND ▼ CUSTOMS

In Japan, they have a festival of dolls. Dolls are brought out to play with on this special day.

HISTORY

Dolls of the 1800s had heads made from china. Their bodies were made of leather or cloth stuffed with sawdust.

Native American children made dolls from corn husks.

DOLL COLLECTIONS

Some people collect dolls for a hobby. In many museums, you can find collections of dolls.

DOLPHIN

SEE ALSO • Animal • Mammal • Whale

A dolphin is a mammal that lives in the ocean. Dolphins come to the surface of the water to breathe.

PARTS OF A BOTTLE-NOSED DOLPHIN

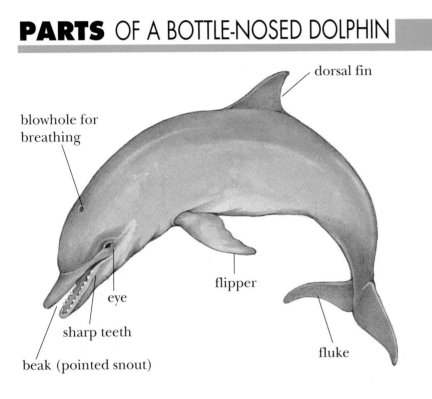

dorsal fin

blowhole for breathing

eye

sharp teeth

beak (pointed snout)

flipper

fluke

Average length: 3.7 metres
Average weight: 180 kilograms

FOOD

fish

shellfish

squid

Scientists think dolphins are very clever animals. Dolphins are friendly and can be trained to act on command. They talk to each other through whistles, barks and clicking sounds.

HOW DOLPHINS LIVE

- A baby dolphin is born in the water.
- The mother and other female dolphins push the young dolphin to the surface for its first breath.
- The mother feeds the young dolphin milk for about one year.

INTERESTING FACT

Dolphins swim in groups called schools.

DRAGON

SEE ALSO • Book • Festival • Heritage

A dragon is not real. It is an imaginary creature. Long ago, people thought dragons were real. They imagined that dragons had four legs, a long tail, scaly skin and wings. People thought that dragons could breathe fire.

Dragons were thought to be evil creatures who lived on mountain tops and had lots of gold. Many stories were told about how dragons ate people and even whole ships.

JAPANESE AND CHINESE DRAGONS

In Japan and China, people believed dragons were beautiful, friendly and wise. Buildings and ornaments were decorated with dragons.

Dragons play an important part in the Chinese New Year. Dragon dancers hope to frighten away evil spirits and bring good luck at Chinese New Year.

DRAGONFLY

SEE ALSO • Animal • Insect • Pond Life

A dragonfly is an insect. Dragonflies can be seen flying over ponds and rivers in summer. They help people by eating harmful insects such as mosquitoes.

PARTS OF A DRAGONFLY

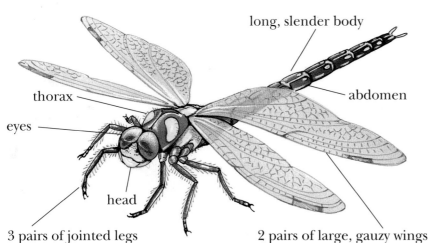

long, slender body

thorax

abdomen

eyes

head

3 pairs of jointed legs

2 pairs of large, gauzy wings

FOOD

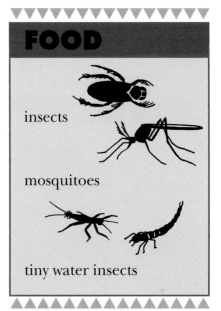

insects

mosquitoes

tiny water insects

HOW A DRAGONFLY LIVES

- A dragonfly mates in flight.
- It lays its eggs in water inside the stems of waterplants.
- The young dragonfly (nymph) hatches and lives underwater using gills to breathe. When fully grown, it climbs a water reed and sheds its skin to emerge as a dragonfly.
- As a dragonfly grows, it sheds its skin 5 to 13 times.

MEALS ON THE WING

As it flies, the dragonfly holds its legs together like a basket to catch insects. It grasps its prey with its legs or jaws, and eats it while flying.

INTERESTING FACT

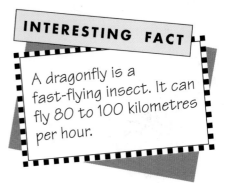

A dragonfly is a fast-flying insect. It can fly 80 to 100 kilometres per hour.

DRAMA

SEE ALSO • Ballet • Dancing • Puppet

Drama tells a story through acting. Drama is performed before an audience. Actors pretend to be other people, animals or things.

Actors show how the characters feel by talking and moving.

KINDS OF DRAMA

- A tragedy is a sad, serious play.
- A comedy is a funny play with a happy ending.
- Sometimes, you can have a drama which is a sad, but funny play.

A PLAY

A drama performance is called a play. The actors' words are written in a script. Actors memorize the script.

To stage a play, you ▶ need actors and a space in which to perform. You may also need make-up, scenery, props, costumes and lighting.

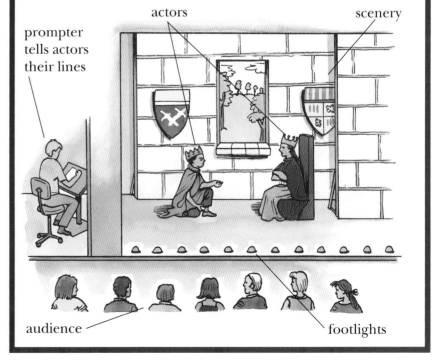

PERFORMING DRAMA

prompter tells actors their lines

actors

scenery

audience

footlights

DRUG

A drug is used to cure disease. Drugs are the medicine doctors give us. A doctor gives drugs to prevent, treat or cure a disease.

| SEE ALSO | • Ambulance • Doctor • Hospital |

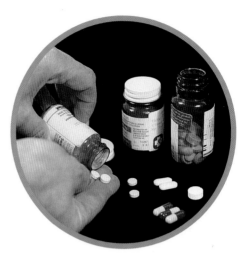

HISTORY

Long ago, most drugs came from plants and herbs. In the 1800s, people made drugs from chemicals.

Penicillin was discovered in 1928 by Alexander Fleming. It was the first drug that could fight bacteria which caused disease.

KINDS OF DRUGS

Many kinds of drugs are used to treat and cure diseases.
• You can swallow drugs or inhale them.
• Drugs can be injected into your body through your skin.
• Skin patches can be placed on your skin. The drug is absorbed through the skin.
• Some drugs are creams and gels. They are rubbed on to the skin.

DRUG ADDICTION

Drugs can be dangerous. A drug addict is a person who takes drugs all the time. They find it hard to live without the drug they are addicted to.

DUCK

SEE ALSO • Animal • Bird • Farming

A duck is a bird. Ducks live near lakes, rivers, marshes and the ocean. Geese and swans are members of the duck family.

PARTS OF A DUCK

probing bill for finding food

long neck for diving

waterproof feathers

tail

3-toed webbed feet for paddling

thin legs for paddling

A MALLARD DUCK

Average weight:
0.5 to 4 kilograms
Average height:
60 centimetres

FOOD

Small water animals (snails)

plants

insects – young beetles, bugs, dragonflies

Saltwater ducks eat shrimps, mussels and sea snails.

HOW DUCKS LIVE

• Ducks live in flocks. The female duck makes a nest in a clump of grass, a hollow or a hole in a tree, and lays 10 to 12 eggs in the nest.
• Ducklings hatch after three to four weeks. Most ducklings can run, swim and find food on the day they hatch. They grow feathers at one month and learn to fly in five to eight weeks.

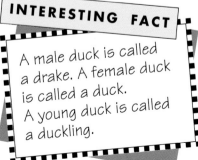

INTERESTING FACT

A male duck is called a drake. A female duck is called a duck. A young duck is called a duckling.